D0459580

Egypt

Come on a journey of discovery

Elaine Jackson

QEB Publishing, Inc.

QEB

Copyright © QEB Publishing, Inc. 2004

Published in the United States by
QEB Publishing
23062 La Cadena Drive
Laguna Hills
Irvine
CA 92653

Library of Congress Control Number 2004101781

ISBN 1-59566-059-3

Written by Elaine Jackson
Designed by Starry Dog Books Ltd
Editor Christine Harvey
Map by PCGraphics (UK) Ltd

Creative Director Louise Morley
Editorial Manager Jean Coppendale

Picture credits

Key: t = top, b = bottom, m = middle, c = center,
l = left, r = right

Corbis Maher Attar 25t,/ Yann Arthur-Bertrand 16–17,/ Bojan Breceli 23m,/ Lloyd Cluff 27m,/ Dean Conger 18,/ Carl and Ann Durcell 16–17m,/ Neema Frederic 24,/ Michelle Garrett 9t,/ Richard Holmes 9b,/ Ed Kashi 8–9,/ Steve Lindridge 26t,/ Michael Nicholson 25m,/ Richard T. Nowitz 7t,/ Nevada Weir 14–15m,/ Jim Winkley 19t,/ Roger Wood 18–19, 25b;
Getty John Chard 6–7,/ Aef-Yves Debay 12–13,/ Will and Deni Mcintire 13t, 20–21,/ Jon Gray 10–11,/ Slede Preis 11b,/ James Strachan 26–27;
Image Bank Michael Melford 21m;
Panos Mark Henley 22–23.

International and regional boundaries in areas of dispute and conflict are shown as a simplification of the true situation. This simplification has been undertaken because this book is aimed at the 7–11 age group.

Printed and bound in China

Words in **bold** are explained in the Glossary on page 28.

Contents

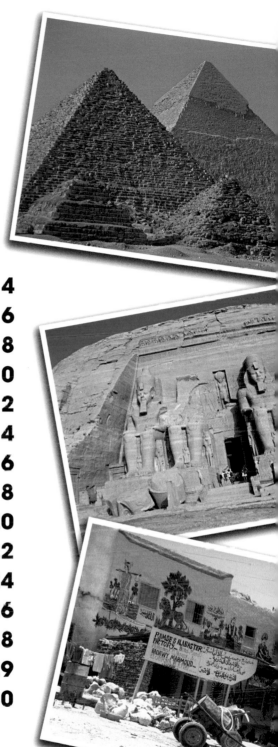

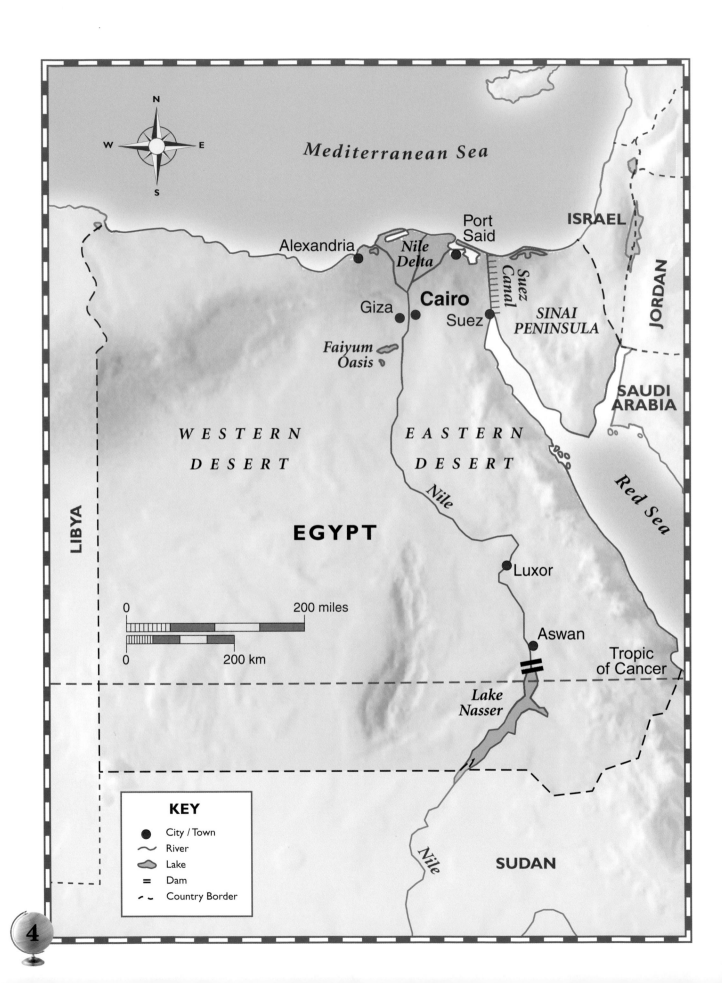

Mediterranean Sea

Port Said

ISRAEL

Alexandria

Nile Delta

JORDAN

Cairo

Suez Canal

Giza

Suez

SINAI PENINSULA

Faiyum Oasis

SAUDI ARABIA

WESTERN DESERT

EASTERN DESERT

Red Sea

Nile

LIBYA

EGYPT

Luxor

Aswan

Tropic of Cancer

Lake Nasser

Nile

SUDAN

0   200 miles

0   200 km

KEY

● City / Town

〜 River

◠ Lake

= Dam

- - Country Border

4

Where in the world is Egypt?

Most of Egypt is on the **continent** of Africa. However, the eastern region of Egypt, the Sinai **Peninsula**, is located on the continent of Asia.

To the east of Egypt is the state of Israel and the Red Sea, to the south is Sudan, to the west is Libya, and to the north is the Mediterranean Sea.

Egypt is about three times as big as the state of New Mexico. However, 95 percent of the land is covered by desert, so people cannot live there. This means that most of Egypt's population squashes into just 3 percent of the country's land.

▼ Egypt and its place in the world.

Egypt

The national flag of Egypt

Did you know?

Official name
Arab Republic of Egypt
Location
Northeast Africa
Surrounding countries
Sudan, Libya, State of Israel
Surrounding seas
Mediterranean Sea, Red Sea
Length of coastline 1,522 miles
Capital city Cairo
Area 386,681 square miles
Population 70,300,000
Life expectancy Male: 63, Female: 66
Religions Islam (94%), Christian (6%)
Official language Arabic (English and French widely understood by educated people)
Climate Desert. Hot, dry summers with moderate winters
Highest mountains
Mount Catherine (8,625 ft.)
Mount Sinai (7,497 ft.)
Major river
Nile River (length: 900 miles in Egypt; total length: 3,461 miles)
Currency Egyptian pound

What is Egypt like?

A land in the desert
Traveling through Egypt you will see a mixture of old and new; mud brick villages and ancient ruins, surrounded by modern city buildings of glass and steel. Some people will be wearing jeans or suits, others traditional robes.

The Nile River
The Nile flows through the entire length of the country from south to north. On each side of the river there is a green strip of rich farmland surrounded by vast deserts.

The Western Desert
West of the Nile River is the area known as the Western Desert. This covers two-thirds of Egypt. It is a low-lying area of endless sand and **sand dunes**, with some stony plains. Very few people live in this desert.

The Eastern Desert
This is also called the Arabian Desert. It lies to the east of the Nile River. Most of the Eastern Desert is uninhabited. There are a few settlements along the

◀ This desert canyon in Sinai contains spectacular natural rock sculptures.

▼ There are two islands in the Nile in Cairo, which are linked to the mainland by bridges. Below is Roda (Rawdah), the other island is called Zamalik.

Red Sea coast to the east, where some people live around wells and springs, to be near a water source.

Green areas in the desert

In the desert there are areas of land where plants and trees grow well and lakes are formed. These areas are called **oases** and are important for farming.

▶ The young girl is selling shells at Lake Qurun, in the Faiyum Oasis.

▼ Most of Egypt is covered in desert.

Mediterranean Sea

MEDITERRANEAN COAST

ISRAEL

JORDAN

Nile Delta

Suez Canal

Cairo ●

Faiyum Oasis

SINAI PENINSULA

LIBYA

WESTERN DESERT
(Libyan Desert/ Egyptian Sahara)

NILE VALLEY

EASTERN DESERT

Nile

Red Sea

EGYPT

Lake Nasser

SUDAN

Nile

Tom's dad is living in Egypt for six months. He is working for an Egyptian chemical company. Tom often receives postcards from the places his dad has visited.

Dear Tom,
This post card shows Mount Sinai, where God is thought to have delivered the Ten Commandments to Moses. It is on the Sinai Peninsula. Tomorrow I am going to Mount Katherine, Egypt's highest point.
Love, Dad

Tom Smith
1562 Elm St.
Townsville,
OH 34602
USA

Dear Tom,
This is the Faiyum Depression in the Western Desert. It is the most important oasis in Egypt. The large freshwater lake lies 174 ft. below sea level!
Love, Dad

Tom Smith
1562 Elm St.
Townsville,
OH 34602
USA

Dear Tom,
Today I visited the Mediterranean coast. There are lots of beautiful white sandy beaches. Egyptian families living in Cairo come here to escape the heat of the city. Me, too!
Love, Dad

Tom Smith
1562 Elm St.
Townsville,
OH 34602
USA

7

Food and drink

Eating in Egypt

Egypt's location—at the crossroads where Africa meets Asia—influences the type of food Egyptians like to eat.

In Egypt, you will eat meals full of the fresh ingredients that are grown in this country. These include different types of beans, which are eaten either stewed or ground up to make pastes such as **hummus**—with lots of garlic. **Okra**, cabbage, eggplant, and potatoes are eaten frequently, often cooked with tomatoes and garlic. You will eat a lot of tomatoes in Egypt—Egyptians love them! Rice is always available and is even eaten for breakfast.

▼ A weekly vegetable market is held in Qutur village in the Nile delta.

Meat and fish

Lamb and chicken are the most common meats in Egypt. They are usually broiled or roasted. Shish kebabs, which are pieces of meat and vegetables cooked on sticks, are extremely popular and are often served with side dishes such as tomato salad and pita bread. Egyptians also enjoy fish, such as perch and tuna, caught in the Red Sea.

Dear Tom,
I had a wonderful meal last night. It was Egyptian moussaka with cheese topping. The side salad was delicious. It was made with chopped tomatoes, cilantro, mint, some hot green peppers, and onions. I had some hot pita bread with it. I'll have to make it for you when I get home. I'm eating lots of fresh fruit, such as figs, dates, oranges, and pomegranates. Speaking of fruit, there is a great cold drink made from fresh-squeezed oranges and sweetened with cut sugarcane. It is just what I need in this hot climate.

Love, Dad

Tom Smith
1562 Elm St.
Townsville,
OH 34602
USA

▲ A family meal of shish kebabs and potatoes.

▼ Spice merchants like to **haggle**.

Climate — traveling through the seasons

Hot and dry

No matter what time of year you travel to Egypt, you will probably find it very hot and dry. It is like this for most of the year. During the winter months, December through February, the average daily temperatures are around 68°F in the north and 79°F in the south.

Spring

Between March and April, the *khamsin*, a dry, hot, dusty wind, blows in from the Western Desert. It can reach a speed of 93 miles per hour! The sky turns dark orange and gets full of dust. Even though everyone closes their doors and windows tightly, the inside of every house gets covered with sand.

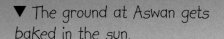

▼ *The ground at Aswan gets baked in the sun.*

Summer

Summer in Egypt is very hot. The temperature is over 88°F most days. The highest temperature recorded in Aswan, in southern Egypt, was over 122°F! Aswan does not receive much rainfall and is almost bone-dry. A lot of water from the Nile and also from Lake Nasser (an artificial lake on the Nile River) evaporates in the hot air.

Tom's dad visited Aswan in July and said it was very hot. Tom looked on the Internet to find out what the climates are like in Aswan and Cairo.

CLIMATE DATA FOR ASWAN (°F)											
Jan	Feb	March	April	May	June	July	Aug	Sep	Oct	Nov	Dec
59	63	68	77	86	91	93	91	88	84	73	61
CLIMATE DATA FOR CAIRO (°F)											
Jan	Feb	March	April	May	June	July	Aug	Sep	Oct	Nov	Dec
54	57	61	68	75	81	82	82	77	73	66	57

One night while he was in Aswan, Tom's dad couldn't sleep. He decided to record the temperature every hour. Here are his records for July 19.

Midnight	1:00	2:00	3:00	4:00	5:00	6:00	7:00	8:00	9:00	10:00	11:00 a.m.
90°F	88	84	84	82	82	81	81	84	90	93	100
Noon	1:00	2:00	3:00	4:00	5:00	6:00	7:00	8:00	9:00	10:00	11:00 p.m.
102°F	104	106	106	106	106	104	104	100	97	93	91

Compare these temperatures with those in July in your local area

▼ Traditional wood boats called *feluccas*, with cotton sails, glide gacefully past Aswan on the Nile.

❓ What kind of clothes would Tom's dad need for a visit to Aswan?

❓ How would he protect himself from the heat and the sun?

❓ Why do you think many Egyptians wear long flowing white robes?

11

Getting around Egypt

By air
Egypt's airlines fly to many Egyptian destinations as well as to lots of countries around the world.

By land
Egypt is one of the largest countries in Africa. As you travel around Egypt, you will have many types of vehicles to choose from, including cars, buses, trucks, and taxis. Or you can use more old-fashioned forms of transportation, such as camels, donkeys, and horses.

By land
Egypt's railroads connect just about every town in the country, from Aswan to Alexandria. Cairo has the only subway system on the whole continent of Africa.

By boat
For centuries, taking a boat on the Nile River was the best way to travel in Egypt. Today, it is possible to take a tourist boat to cruise up the Nile between Aswan and Luxor. Traditional sailboats, called *feluccas*, still travel on the Nile River.

Suez Canal

The Suez Canal is one of the world's busiest shipping routes. It connects the Red Sea and the Mediterranean Sea. The **canal** was dug between 1859 and 1869. Before that, ships bringing cargo by sea to Europe from India and the Far East had to travel round the whole continent of Africa! The canal is 101 miles long, and the narrowest parts are 197 feet wide. Along most of the canal there is one traffic lane and only a few passing bays.

▲ Downtown Cairo is always busy with traffic.

▼ Ships on the Suez Canal transport goods through Egypt to many other countries worldwide.

Dear Tom,
I really wanted to take a ride along the Nile River, but not on a tourist boat! I took a trip on a felucca. Feluccas are traditional Egyptian boats that do not have an engine. They rely on the breeze, which builds up during the day, to blow their sails.
Love, Dad

Tom Smith
1562 Elm St.
Townsville,
OH 34602
USA

13

The Nile River

Ten-year-old Mohammed goes to school in Cairo. He is working with two friends on a project about the Nile River.

▲ The Nile River, viewed from the air.

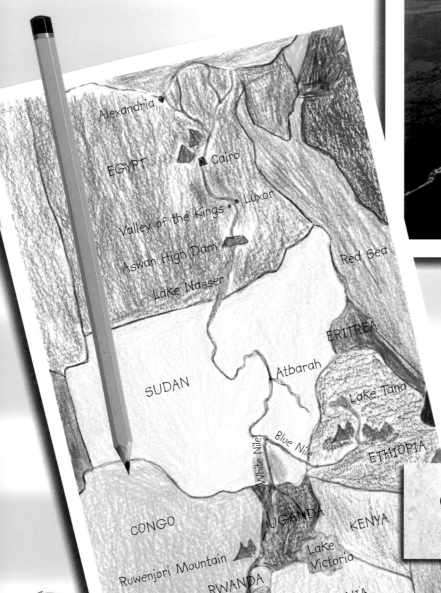

◀ Mohammed's drawing of the Nile shows all the countries it flows through.

Compare the lengths of the Nile and the Mississippi in the U.S.

Mohammed and his classmates have been asked to write about the Nile River as part of a class project.

By Mohammed, age 10

From the Nile's source to about halfway along its length at Khartoum in Sudan, the river is known as the White Nile. This is because of the milky-white color of the water in the summer. At other times the water is brownish-gray and muddy. At Khartoum the river is joined by the Blue Nile, which starts in the mountains of Ethiopia. This is known as the Blue Nile because it is clear and blue during the months of low water from March to June.

By Layla, age 10

The Nile River is the world's longest river. It is a truly international river, since it flows through a total of ten countries. It is 3,461 miles long. This is similar to the distance between New York and London!

It flows from its source in the Ruwenzori Mountains, on Uganda's border with the Democratic Republic of Congo, to its mouth on the Mediterranean Sea in northern Egypt. The Nile's mouth is in northern Egypt at the Mediterranean Sea.

By Ezzat, age 9

Before the Blue Nile and the White Nile meet, they flow side by side for several hundred miles, not mixing. You can actually see the brownish-gray color of the White Nile and the greenish-blue color of the Blue Nile. From Khartoum to the Mediterranean Sea only one river, the Atbara River, joins the Nile. So, unlike most rivers, the Nile River does not get any wider as it nears the sea. Around Cairo, the Nile begins to branch out into its **delta**.

15

Lake Nasser and the Aswan Dam

Lake Nasser

At the point where the Nile River reaches the border of Sudan and Egypt, the river flows into Lake Nasser, the world's biggest man-made lake.

The Aswan Dam

Lake Nasser was created when the Aswan Dam was built in 1971. The **dam** blocked the flow of the Nile. The dam is described as Egypt's modern pyramid. It is 17 times larger than the biggest pyramid.

▼ Lake Nasser is more than 311 miles long, of which 93 miles belong to Sudan and the rest to Egypt.

▼ The Aswan Dam is 2.2 miles long and 364 feet high. It is 3,215 feet wide at the bottom and 131 feet wide at the top.

As part of Mohammed's project on the Nile River, he has recorded the advantages and disadvantages that the building of the Aswan Dam has had for Egypt.

ADVANTAGES AND DISADVANTAGES OF THE ASWAN DAM

ADVANTAGES

1) Controls the flow of the Nile to prevent flooding.
2) Prevents **drought**.
3) Provides a regular supply of water to use for **irrigation**, so crops can be grown all year round.
4) Irrigation increased the amount of land that can be farmed by 30%.
5) Source of energy. The dam produces enough electricity for the whole of Egypt. Its **hydroelectric** power is an energy source that does not create pollution, as oil does.

DISADVANTAGES

1) Thousands of people had to leave their homes to make way for the dam and the lake.
2) Ancient temples and buildings had to be moved, stone by stone, and rebuilt on higher ground.
3) Fewer fish in the Nile because there are fewer **nutrients** in the water, since the dam holds back all the **silt**.
4) Farmers have to buy a lot of expensive chemical fertilizer (natural or chemical substances that make soil produce more crops), because there is no natural fertilizing of the land by silt.
5) The large number of irrigation **canals** has increased diseases such as malaria (an infectious disease that causes chills and fever), which is spread by mosquitoes that breed in still water.
6) Loss of water through high levels of evaporation from the surface of Lake Nasser.

Farming

Growing food

Egypt is totally dependent on the Nile's waters because the country has so little rainfall each year. River water is used for cooking, washing, drinking, and watering **crops**.

The Nile Valley

All along the Nile Valley, a narrow strip of land on each side of the river is farmed. Every available piece of land is **irrigated**, in order to grow food to eat and crops to sell.

In the past, farmers relied on the flood waters from the river, which left behind rich mud that helped the crops to grow. Now people have to use more irrigation and fertilizers, because the Aswan Dam has stopped the Nile flooding as it used to do.

◀ Tossing dry beans high up in the air in a sieve sifts out all the waste and dust.

▼ The land that lies on both sides of the river is irrigated to grow more crops.

◀ Some farmers still use traditional methods, such as this sakia wheel, to water their land.

In Ezzat's school project, he writes about his family. They are farmers who live in the countryside.

By Ezzat, age 9

My uncle and grandpa are fellahins (farmers) and live in a village about 22 miles from Cairo. Their land is a few miles from the Nile River. They grow wheat, corn, and vegetables for the family to eat. They also grow a crop called berseem which they feed to the farm animals. They keep water buffalo, goats, and donkeys on the farm. They also grow rice, sugarcane, dates, and fruit, such as oranges and bananas, to sell.

My grandpa and uncle are lucky, because the irrigation channel (a long ditch) runs next to their fields. They have a pump to lift the water from the channel onto their fields. Some farmers use old methods, such as a shadoof, which is a long pole with a bucket at one end and a weight at the other. The pole is fixed to a post, and the pole swings around so that water from the river can be poured on the fields. Some farmers use animals to turn a wheel called a sakia, which scoops water up and then onto the fields.

Tourism in Egypt

Historical wonders

The tourist trade is very important to the Egyptian economy. Many tourists visit the Nile River and its surrounding area because this is where Egypt's historical treasures are found.

The ancient Egyptians believed that their time on Earth was short, but that the **afterlife** would go on forever. They built huge pyramids to use as burial chambers. Tourists are attracted by the age-old mystery of how and why the pyramids were built and thousands visit them each year.

Ancient cities

If you travel to Egypt, you will probably want to visit Giza, a suburb of Cairo. This is where the Great Pyramids and the huge Sphinx are. Luxor, built on the site of the ancient city of Thebes, is another place you could visit.

People have been coming to visit the impressive temples and monuments of Luxor for thousands of years. The Valley of the Kings, including the spectacular tombs of Tutankhamun and Nefertari, is also a big attraction.

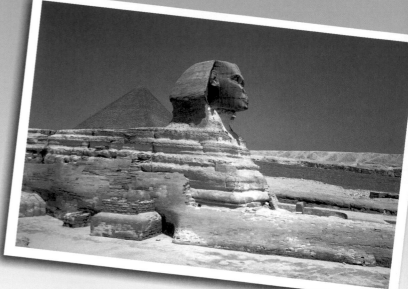

▼ The statue of the Sphinx in Giza, is 72 feet high and 164 feet long. It was built almost 5,000 years ago.

◄ The Great Pyramids are at Giza, on the west bank of the Nile.

Tom went to stay with his dad in Egypt over Christmas vacation. He kept a diary of some of the places he visited.

December 15
Today we went to Giza. Wow! I could not believe my eyes! The Sphinx was so huge! The enormous half-human and half-lion statue rose out of the desert, keeping a watchful eye over the three Great Pyramids. I had never seen anything like it before! I was really seeing one of the Seven Wonders of the World.

December 19
Today dad took me to the Valley of the Kings. We went to Tutankhamun's tomb and looked at the treasures and jewels. They had been buried in his tomb with his mummified body. I knew quite a lot about Tutankhamun because I had done some work on the ancient Egyptians in school.

▲The great temple at Abu Simbel. This temple had to be moved to higher ground in the 1960s or it would have been flooded after the Aswan Dam was built.

▲ Tutankhamun's gold death mask Tutankhamun is probably the most famous ancient Egyptian pharaoh, or King. His treasure-filled burial chamber was discovered in 1922.

Egypt's industries

The **textile industry** is the most important industry in Egypt. Other industries include the production of cement, iron and steel, chemicals, fertilizers, and rubber products.

Mining has become more important in the last 20 years. Raw materials such as oil and salt are taken out of the ground.

Energy isn't a problem in Egypt. The country is **self-sufficient** with oil, and the Aswan Dam provides most of the country's electrical power.

Agriculture

Even though only four percent of Egypt's land area can be farmed, agriculture is important. Egypt **imports** about half of its food, because so much of the farmland is used for the production of cotton.

Some crops grown in Egypt are sold around the world. These include corn, sugarcane, wheat, rice, barley, millet (a grass made into grain and animal food), onions, potatoes, tobacco, mangoes, citrus fruits, figs, dates, and grapes.

Tourism

The tourist industry is very important to Egypt. The country has always been popular with visitors who are interested in the pyramids and the mysteries of the ancient Egyptian civilization.

▶ A cotton merchant in Cairo stands by huge bales of cotton. Egypt is the world's largest **exporter** of this product.

▼ Nile cruises and trips on feluccas are very popular with tourists.

▶ Making fertilizer is an important industry in Egypt. Much of it is used in Egypt itself, and large amounts are exported to surrounding countries.

Cairo

A mixture of old and new

As you travel around Cairo, you will be surprised by the contrasts in the buildings, the methods of transport, and even the types of clothes that people wear. Sometimes you will feel you are in a busy, modern city, and at other times you will feel you have stepped back in history.

Traditional Cairo

Some areas of the city are very traditional. These areas have narrow winding streets, busy markets, covered **bazaars**, and craft workshops. There are many tea- and coffeehouses in these narrow streets. They are very popular.

My name is Ahmed and I live in Cairo, the capital city of Egypt. My city is the largest in Egypt and in the whole of Africa. Almost 25 percent of all Egyptians live here.

24

▼ Cairo's skyline is crowded with modern high-rise buildings and the minarets, or spires of mosques.

▲ Five million people live in Cairo's camps and slums.

▼ Ali and his friend Adio help out at a copper stand.

Cairo's problems

Some areas of the city are very poor. People live in camps and slums, without any decent water supply or **sewage** system. Many people make a living by collecting garbage from the streets, sorting through it, and selling the materials to be recycled.

Cairo has many problems that face urban areas all over the world, such as overcrowding, traffic congestion, air pollution, unemployment, and a lack of good-quality housing.

My name is Ali.
I go to school, but only for half days. This is because there are so many children that the school cannot give us all full-time education. I love to play soccer and go for bike rides. My dad drives a tourist bus and my mom works in our home.

25

Traveling through Egyptian cities

As you travel through Egyptian cities, you will be amazed at the incredible mix of ancient and modern architecture and lifestyles. Egyptian cities, such as Luxor, are sometimes compared to open-air museums with huge numbers of preserved monuments.

However, located not far from these ancient monuments and historic buildings are new buildings and some of the most up-to-date industries. Today, all aspects of modern life can be found in Egypt's cities.

▼ Along its route, the Suez Canal runs through three lakes.

▼ The city of Alexandria once had a lighthouse that was one of the Seven Wonders of the World.

For their school projects, three children have written about their hometowns. They say what makes their towns special, and what they like to do there for fun.

My name is Manal and I live in Port Said. This is a **port** on the Mediterranean Sea at the entrance to the Suez Canal. It is the second largest port in Egypt and a fueling point for ships using the canal. I love to watch the big boats going past. Egyptian products such as cotton and rice are exported from Port Said.

▼ The hydroelectric power station at Aswan provides electricity for all of Egypt.

My name is Elham and I live in Alexandria in northern Egypt. My town is on the Mediterranean Sea, so the climate is cooler than in central Egypt. I am lucky because I can go down to the beach to go swimming. My uncle, aunt, and cousin Ahmed, who live in Cairo, have a vacation home here in Alexandria, right on the waterfront. We have lots of fun playing on the sandy beaches. There are lots of hotels and apartments in Alexandria for tourists.
Alexandria is also Egypt's leading port and is a modern industrial city.

My name is Rashid. I live in the city of Suez at the southern end of the Suez Canal. Suez is a fueling station for ships and a center for storing oil. Oil is sent by pipelines to Cairo and Alexandria. Petroleum products, paper, and fertilizers are made in Suez. My friends and I like to see all the ships refueling.

Glossary

afterlife
life after death

bazaar
a market, often covered

canal
a manmade water channel for navigation or irrigation

continent
one of the seven large areas of land on the earth's surface: Africa, Asia, Australia, Antarctica, North America, South America, Europe

crop
a plant grown for food or raw materials

dam
a manmade barrier across a river, which blocks its flow and creates a lake behind it

delta
area of flat land at the mouth of a river, criss-crossed by many small channels

drought
period when no rain falls

exports
goods sold to other countries

haggle
to bargain over a price

hummus
food made from chickpeas and sesame seed paste

hydroelectric power (HEP)
electricity made from the controlled flow of water

imports
goods brought into a country from other countries to use and sell

industry
making things in factories or workshops

irrigation
taking water onto land from a river, using a system of canals and channels

nutrients
nourishing vitamins and mineral substances

oasis (plural oases)
fertile place in the desert where there is water, and trees grow

okra
green vegetable also called "ladies' fingers"

peninsula
land surrounded on three sides by water

plateau (plural plateaux)
a wide, level stretch of land high above sea level

port
a place where ships stop to load and unload their cargo and passengers

sand dunes
rounded ridges of drifted sand

self-sufficient
able to provide for oneself

sewage
waste liquid from toilets, houses, or factories

silt
fine fragments of soil and rock carried down by a river

source
where a river or stream starts

textile
fabric or cloth, usually woven

urban
living in, or situated in, a large town or city

Index

Teaching ideas and activities for children

The **Travel Through** series offers up-to-date information and interdisciplinary knowledge in subject areas such as geography, language arts, mathematics, history, and social studies. The series enables children to develop an overview ("the big picture") of each country. This overview reflects the huge diversity and richness of the life and culture of each country. The series aims to prevent the development of misconceptions, stereotypes, and prejudices, which often develop when the focus of a study narrows too quickly onto a small locality within a country. The books will help children gain access to this overview, and also develop an understanding of the interconnectedness of places. They contribute to children's geographical knowledge, skills, and understanding, and help them to make sense of the world around them.

A: ACTIVITIES TO DEVELOP THINKING SKILLS
ACTIVITIES TO PROMOTE RESEARCH AND RECALL OF FACTS
Ask the children to:
• make an alphabet book for a young child, reflecting what places in Egypt are like (for example, physical and manmade features, weather, industry).
• research and investigate a desert environment. Ask the children to present their information on a poster or in a photo journal.

ACTIVITIES TO PROMOTE UNDERSTANDING
• Ask the children to use this book and other nonfiction books, CD-ROMs, and the Internet to find out about farming and industry in Egypt, and then use this information to make a children's TV documentary program.

ACTIVITIES TO PROMOTE THE USE OF KNOWLEDGE AND SKILLS TO SOLVE PROBLEMS

Ask the children to:

• work in groups to produce a poster advertising different types of vacations to Egypt.

• make notes to explain why the Nile Valley is so heavily populated but other areas of Egypt are not. List the attributes of the Nile River.

ACTIVITIES TO ENCOURAGE ANALYTICAL THINKING

• Ask the children to reflect on what the issues would be if Egypt's population doubled within the next five years.

ACTIVITIES TO PROMOTE CREATIVITY

Ask the children to:

• make a representation of the desert areas through painting or collage.

• design an itinerary for a cruise ship on the Nile River, including onboard activities and onshore excursions to places of interest.

ACTIVITIES TO HELP CHILDREN USE EVIDENCE TO FORM OPINIONS AND EVALUATE CONSEQUENCES OF DECISIONS

Ask the children to:

• rank the places in Egypt they would like to visit in order of preference, giving reasons.

• write a report, giving reasons, about who in Egypt benefited from the building of the Aswan Dam and who did not.

B: ACTIVITIES BASED ON DIFFERENT LEARNING STYLES

ACTIVITIES FOR LINGUISTIC LEARNERS

Ask the children to:

• write a rap to promote a cruise on the Nile River as a great vacation.

• write a journalistic report about the impact of too many tourists visiting the pyramids.

ACTIVITIES FOR LOGICAL AND MATHEMATICAL LEARNERS

Ask the children to:

• find out about the population of Egypt or Cairo over the past ten years, collate this information, and represent it in a number of graphical ways.

• find ways of graphically representing the information about climate in this book.

ACTIVITIES FOR VISUAL LEARNERS

Ask the children to:

• design a poster or cartoon to show a visit to the pyramids and a ride on a camel.

• select one place in Egypt and design a visually appealing poster, with a slogan, that could be used to advertise that place.

• draw their favorite place in Egypt on the front of a post card-size piece of cardboard or poster paper.

ACTIVITIES FOR KINESTHETIC LEARNERS

Ask the children to:

• make a model of the Nile River from its source to the mouth.

• design and build a model of a pyramid, a temple, or the Sphinx.

ACTIVITIES FOR MUSICAL LEARNERS

Ask the children to:

• create an Egyptian dance.

• create a short radio commercial and radio jingle to advertise a place or tourist attraction in Egypt.

ACTIVITIES FOR INTERPERSONAL LEARNERS

Ask the children to:

• write a letter to a child living in Cairo, explaining their own lifestyle (school, hobbies, local area).

• plan an imaginary visit to Egypt for their family.

ACTIVITIES FOR INTRAPERSONAL LEARNERS

Ask the children to:

• describe what they feel it would be like to live in Aswan.

• describe how they would feel riding a camel.

ACTIVITIES FOR NATURALISTIC LEARNERS

Ask the children to:

• make notes about the pros and cons of expanding farmland into the desert through the use of irrigation and underground water reservoirs.

• discuss the effect of the Aswan Dam on the plants, animals, and fish in the Nile Valley and delta.